W9-BHG-538

AMAZING TRAINS

City Trains

METRO

by Christina Leighton

BLASTOFF! READERS

BELLWETHER MEDIA • MINNEAPOLIS, MN

Note to Librarians, Teachers, and Parents:

Blastoff! Readers are carefully developed by literacy experts and combine standards-based content with developmentally appropriate text.

Level 1 provides the most support through repetition of high-frequency words, light text, predictable sentence patterns, and strong visual support.

Level 2 offers early readers a bit more challenge through varied simple sentences, increased text load, and less repetition of high-frequency words.

Level 3 advances early-fluent readers toward fluency through increased text and concept load, less reliance on visuals, longer sentences, and more literary language.

Level 4 builds reading stamina by providing more text per page, increased use of punctuation, greater variation in sentence patterns, and increasingly challenging vocabulary.

Level 5 encourages children to move from "learning to read" to "reading to learn" by providing even more text, varied writing styles, and less familiar topics.

Whichever book is right for your reader, Blastoff! Readers are the perfect books to build confidence and encourage a love of reading that will last a lifetime!

This edition first published in 2018 by Bellwether Media, Inc.

No part of this publication may be reproduced in whole or in part without written permission of the publisher. For information regarding permission, write to Bellwether Media, Inc., Attention: Permissions Department, 5357 Penn Avenue South, Minneapolis, MN 55419.

Library of Congress Cataloging-in-Publication Data

Names: Leighton, Christina, author.
Title: City Trains / by Christina Leighton.
Description: Minneapolis, MN : Bellwether Media, Inc., [2018] | Series:
  Blastoff! Readers: Amazing Trains | Includes bibliographical references
  and index. | Audience: Age 5-8. | Audience: Grade K to 3.
Identifiers: LCCN 2016052932 (print) | LCCN 2017010604 (ebook) | ISBN
  9781626176690 (hardcover : alk. paper) | ISBN 9781681033990 (ebook)
Subjects: LCSH: Street-railroads–Juvenile literature. | Subways–Juvenile
  literature. | Local transit–Juvenile literature.
Classification: LCC HE4211 .L455 2018 (print) | LCC HE4211 (ebook) | DDC
  625.4–dc23
LC record available at https://lccn.loc.gov/2016052932

Editor: Nathan Sommer   Designer: Lois Stanfield

Printed in the United States of America, North Mankato, MN.

Table of Contents

WHAT ARE CITY TRAINS?

City trains carry **passengers** around big cities. They make travel easier for millions of people.

These trains take people to school, work, and many other places every day.

Most city trains use **electricity**. Others have **diesel engines**.

electricity

55 Mall of America

101

The trains can run
in bad weather.
They power through
snow and rain!

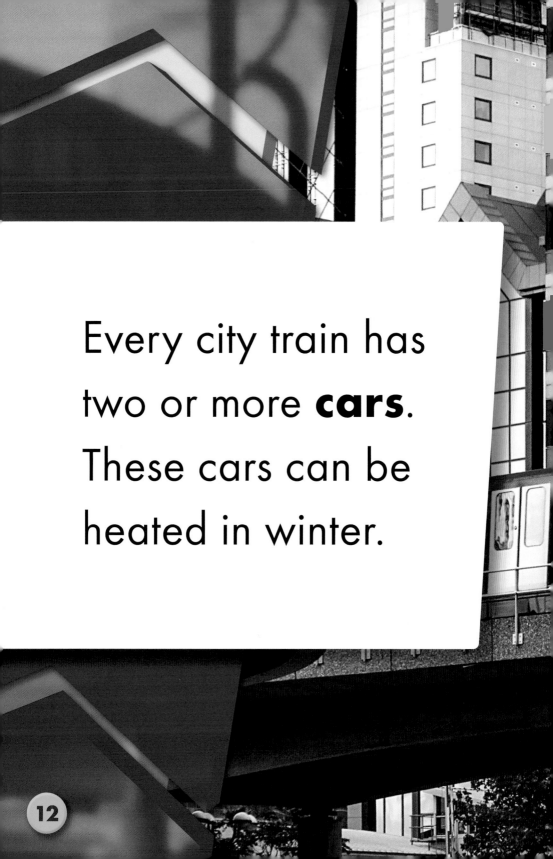

Every city train has two or more **cars**. These cars can be heated in winter.

cars

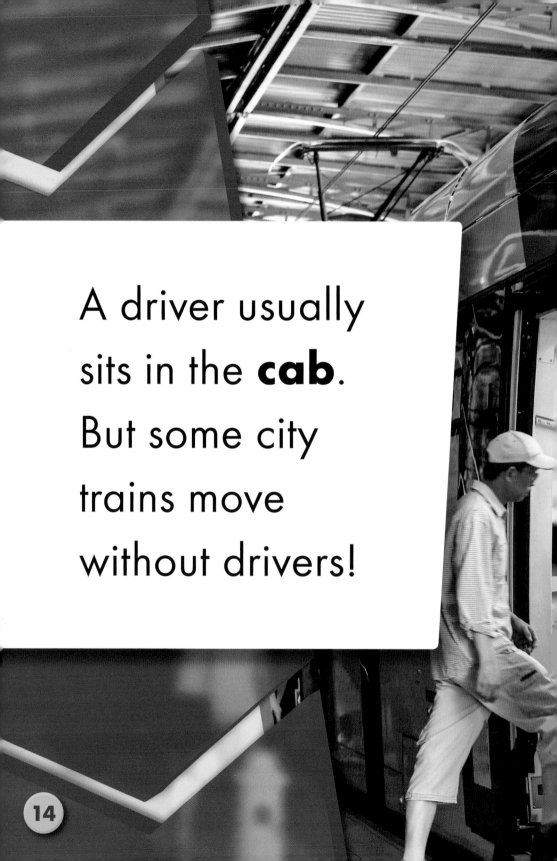

A driver usually sits in the **cab**. But some city trains move without drivers!

cab

Many big cities use city trains. The trains make stops along different paths.

These trains go through **tunnels**. They also cross streets and bridges.

CITY TRAIN PATHS

How many stops does each train make?

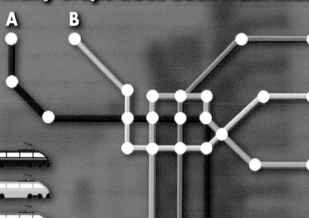

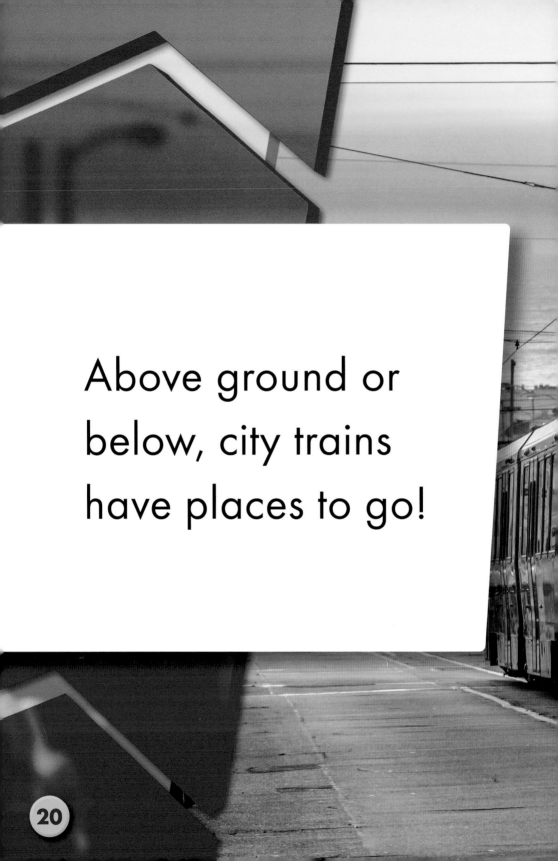

Above ground or below, city trains have places to go!

Glossary

cab

the part of a train where a driver sits

electricity

a form of energy that gives power

cars

vehicles pulled by a train

passengers

people who ride a vehicle to get from one place to another

diesel engines

loud engines that burn diesel fuel

tunnels

dug-out paths that trains travel through

To Learn More

AT THE LIBRARY

Clapper, Nikki Bruno. *City Trains*. North Mankato, Minn.: Capstone Press, 2016.

Klein, Adria. *City Train*. North Mankato, Minn.: Stone Arch Books, 2013.

McBriarty, Patrick T., and Johanna H. Kim. *City Railways Go Above and Below*. Carlisle, Mass.: Applewood Books, 2016.

ON THE WEB

Learning more about city trains is as easy as 1, 2, 3.

1. Go to www.factsurfer.com.

2. Enter "city trains" into the search box.

3. Click the "Surf" button and you will see a list of related web sites.

With factsurfer.com, finding more information is just a click away.

Index

The images in this book are reproduced through the courtesy of: dszc, front cover; Scanrail1, pp. 2-3; PomInOz, pp. 4-5; Transport for London/ Alamy, pp. 6-7; sequential5, pp. 8-9; Official, pp. 10-11; Christopher Dodge, pp. 12-13; imamember, pp. 14-15; BeyondImages, pp. 16-17; CHEN MIN CHUN, pp. 18-19; tovovan, p. 19 (train graphic); Spondylolithesis, pp. 20-21; Agencja Fotograficzna Caro/ Alamy, p. 22 (top left); ChameleonsEye, p. 22 (top right); M DOGAN, p. 22 (center left); Tooykrub, p. 22 (center right); Leonid Andronov, p. 22 (bottom left); Shchipkova Elena, p. 22 (bottom right).